Immagine & Poesia

"La pittura è una poesia che si vede e non si sente, e la poesia è una pittura che si sente e non si vede"
"Painting is poetry that is seen rather than felt, and poetry is painting that is felt rather than seen"

—Leonardo da Vinci, "Trattato della Pittura"

Immagine & Poesia

The Movement in Progress

Poems by Lidia Chiarelli

Artworks by

Alessandro Actis (fine art photos)
Gianpiero Actis (mixed-media paintings)
R Gopakumar (digital art)
Adel Gorgy (fine art photos)
Carolyn Mary Kleefeld (mixed-media painting)
Marsha Solomon (pen-and-ink painting)

Cross-Cultural Communications
Merrick, New York

Some of the poems have previously appeared (or will appear) in
The Seventh Quarry Swansea Poetry Magazine (Wales, UK),
Cross-Cultural Communications Art & Poetry Broadside Series (USA),
Voices Israel (Israel), *Poezia* (Romania, Tr. Olimpia Jacobs).
The editors and publishers are gratefully acknowledged.

Editor-Publisher: **Stanley H. Barkan**

Cross-Cultural Communications
239 Wynsum Avenue
Merrick, NY 11566-4725 USA
Tel: (516) 868-5635 / Fax: (516) 379-1901
cccpoetry@aol.com / cccbarkan@optonline.net
www.cross-culturalcommunication.com

Library of Congress Control Number: 2013942403

ISBN 978-0-89304-994-2

First Edition

Back cover photo by Cesare Dellafiore
Designed by Tchouki
Printed in Bulgaria by Fatum Ltd.

INDICE – CONTENTS

RINGRAZIAMENTI – ACKNOWLEDGMENTS

Tutta la mia gratitudine e il mio affetto a quanti mi hanno aiutata e sostenuta nella realizzazione del Movimento **Immagine & Poesia** e nella creazione di questo libro.

My deepest gratitude and love to all I acknowledge here for their help and support in developing the artistic literary Movement **Immagine & Poesia** and for their confidence in my work:

-    Gianpiero and Alessandro Actis, my talented and emotionally supportive husband and son
-    Adel Gorgy, Mary Gorgy and Marsha Solomon, my chosen American family, for their constant support and for the significant difference they have made in my life
-    Stanley H. Barkan, my guardian angel and publisher
-    Carolyn Mary Kleefeld (California, U.S.A.), R Gopakumar (India), Marit Risto Fagerly (Norway), Aicha Skandrani (Tunisia), talented artists and enthusiastic representatives of the Movement in their countries
-    Lilita Conrieri, Sandrina Piras and Peter Thabit Jones, and Maria Fiorenza Verde talented poets and my loving friends
-    Gavin Adam Wood, the official songwriter and singer of **Immagine & Poesia**
-    Tchouki (Stoyan Tchoukanov), talented artist and graphic designer of this book
-    Raffaella Spada and her association *Arte Città Amica* that have hosted several of our exhibitions
-    Enzo Papa, the first art critic of the Movement
-    Giada Diano, the Italian biographer of Lawrence Ferlinghetti for her support of our project
-    The associations *Gli Amici di Guido Gozzano* and *Salotto Letterario* for their creative support

-    In memory of my beloved friend and muse, Aeronwy Thomas

Above all, thanks to **Lawrence Ferlinghetti** and **Ugo Nespolo** who have honored our Movement with their precious contributions and whose poetry and art continually inspire me.

PRESENTAZIONE

"Ut pictura poesis" , "la pittura è come la poesia", una locuzione formulata da Orazio circa due mila anni fa ("Ars Poetica" – "Epistola ad Pisones") che fa ancora discutere.

Il paragone tra le due forme espressive è da sempre dibattuto per metterne in risalto le analogie e le differenze che intercorrono tra di esse. E mentre la pittura è il linguaggio che sancisce l'espressività della figurazione, la poesia recupera quella del *logos,* della parola. Una dialettica che sta alla base di questa pubblicazione e che mette a confronto poesie, raffigurazioni pittoriche, fotografie, disegni a penna e arte digitale di diversi artisti.

Le 21 liriche della torinese Lidia Chiarelli, fanno da filo conduttore a tutto il libro, e ad esse si legano, si confrontano e si contrappongono tutte le altre figurazioni: gli acrilici di Gianpiero Actis, le fotografie di Alessandro Actis e quelle dell'americano Adel Gorgy; oppure le figurazioni prodotte con varie tecniche dalle americane Carolyn Mary Kleefeld e Marsha Solomon e dall'indiano Gopakumar.

Una partita aperta tra artisti di varia caratura e di varie nazionalità che rende il confronto allettante e singolare. Da una parte i sentimenti, i ricordi, le nostalgie di luoghi e atmosfere, dall'altra l'atto della pittura, del segno e della figurazione. E' in questo territorio, che possiamo definire dell'astrazione, che avviene l'incontro tra le varie arti in gioco, com'è nello spirito del Movimento artistico – letterario "Immagine & Poesia".

Il volume si apre con un omaggio poetico e figurativo a Jackson Pollock. Una lirica di Lidia Chiarelli, bilanciata dalla fotografia di una produzione del grande esponente dell'Action Painting (Pittura d'azione), realizzata da Adel Gorgy. L'alfabeto si mescola al gestualismo, la tensione del gesto si fa parola e Chiarelli può dire, visitando la Pollock - Krasner house: *"Ora finalmente/ posso vederti/ Jackson Pollock/ chino sul pavimento/... intento a sgocciolare colori sulla tela".*

Inizia da qui il diario di un vagabondaggio pittorico e letterario, che si trasforma lungo le sue tappe in un reportage multimediale a più mani, su ricordi, nostalgie, descrizioni di luoghi e metropoli, che mette a confronto pittura, fotografia, disegni, arte digitale e poesia, coinvolgendo emotivamente il fruitore.

Cito una delle tappe più intriganti: "Times Square", una lirica in cui Chiarelli chiede alle luci della più famosa piazza di New York di accendersi ancora una volta per lei: "Accendetevi/ accendetevi ancora una volta/ luci di Times Square/ Accendetevi per me/ in quest'ultima sera a New York/ L'aria calda delle strade è un manto leggero/ che mi avvolge"... /Lasciate che i miei occhi/ si perdano/ ancora / nel vostro vortice / dolce e inebriante".

Sul versante della figurazione, in particolare della pittura di Gianpiero Actis, c'è una partecipazione espressiva che non è imitazione della natura, non è arte di semplice visione, ma trasposizione di sentimenti attraverso il colore che spesso diventa ricerca di stile, come accade per la fotografia e per gli altri media, ciascuno dei quali andrebbe studiato e compreso ognuno per il suo verso e confrontato con la poesia, come suggeriva Orazio nella su "Ars Poetica" - "Epistola ad Pisones", che resta ancora uno dei testi di riferimento fondamentali sull'estetica.

—**Francesco Prestipino**
Torino, 2013

FOREWORD

The poems in Lidia Chiarelli's impressive debut collection, *Immagine & Poesia*, remind us that each human being is a universe complete—with suns and moons, eclipses, tidal pulls, and dry deserts—and art is the telescope that allows us to see into other universes.

As Emily Dickinson wrote, "forever is composed of nows," and these intimate, carefully examined and faithfully rendered verses convey a portrait-like quality, presenting portraits of a moment. These are Impressionist paintings of poems—acutely observed, vividly and delicately rendered celebrations of the moments of beauty that surround and permeate us.

Physical sensations combine with emotion and reflection to imbue each work with multiple layers of meaning. The imagery is varyingly dramatic, precise, concrete, cosmopolitan or bucolic, expressing a sense of place and atmosphere. Each poem, each line is meticulously constructed and polished, and each is a work of art that imparts sensations to and summons responses from the reader. Beyond the descriptive, there is an evocation of wonder, loss, exhilaration, tenderness, fear—all those things that make the human experience familiar to all of us. The more personal, the more universal.

Sometimes, as in all our experiences, there are darker passages, as in "Garden in May"

> *The tired petals*
> *on the stones of the path*
> *will form*
> *the drawing of this uncertain time*
> *that the wind will continue to break down*
> *in a ruthless game.*
>
> *It will be the time*
> *when*
> *even the swallows*
>
> *(in rapid elliptic flights*
> *in the pearl sky)*
>
> *come and play again*
> *unaware*
> *of their fate*

But there is also whimsy, as in "Tiffany" wonder, in "Manhattan" and "Niagara," and surprising turnabouts, as when, in "Winter Concert," after

. . . Dazzling
the lights of the shop-windows
give way, and
the city
oddly empty
wraps us up in a damp embrace.

How different would that city and that moment be, if the embrace were cold or warm, or anything other than damp?

But on the whole, these are joyous works, expressing optimism and love of life, as in "The Rest of the Boats,"

Unplanned destinations
stood out in front of us
when
strong and safe
we left to challenge the wind.

Through these pages, the poet's mind wanders freely as the wind, reaching *unplanned destinations*, touching all aspects of life, and that which can scarcely be contained by sails can only be truly captured in poetry and art.

This collection is organized into six sections, offering reflections on Images and Poetry, childhood, the seasons, the rhythm of life, travel, and ending with a special poem dedicated to Lidia's friend and fellow poet, Aeronwy Thomas. Each poem is presented alongside a work of art, created or selected by the artist for it.

Lidia Chiarelli has devoted much of her time to founding and furthering the artistic and literary movement, Immagine & Poesia, which brings together for collaboration, publication and exhibition the works of poets and artists from all over the world. Her sense that art and poetry motivate one another is deeply rooted and actively lived—her husband, Gianpiero Actis is an accomplished painter.

The success of this idea can be witnessed in the absolute harmony of the poems in the collection and the accompanying works of art by painter, Gianpiero Actis, photographer, Alessandro Actis, photographer Adel Gorgy, painter Carolyn Mary Kleefeld, painter Marsha Solomon, and painter Gopakumar. Each of these pairings is a conscious and deliberate collaborative effort; works inspired and informed by each other or chosen expressly for each other. The artworks are not to be understood as illustrations for the poems, nor are the poems captions for the pictures. They are compound artworks composed of, as the movement states, images and poetry.

The poems in Images and Poetry stand securely on their own, however. Singly and collectively, these are works of great originality and lyricism, evincing a profound awareness, as the author points out the beauty inherent in the time and place which we, wherever and whenever we are, call home.

Henry David Thoreau wrote, "music is perpetual, and only the hearing is intermittent." Is it hearing, or is it listening? T. S. Eliot spoke in "Little Gidding" of the discoveries

Not known, because not looked for
But heard, half-heard, in the stillness
Between two waves of the sea.

In these graceful, sensitive poems, Lidia Chiarelli looks and listens. She tunes in to the music of the universe and invites us to hear.

—Mary Gorgy
Long Island, New York
2013

INTRODUZIONE - INTRODUCTION

"Poesia e arte figurativa portano a momenti di creatività incrociata"

Quando la scrittrice inglese **Aeronwy Thomas** (figlia di **Dylan Thomas**) pronunciò queste parole durante la sua visita a Torino nel 2006, nessuno avrebbe potuto immaginare dove questa affermazione ci avrebbe portati. L'anno successivo nasceva infatti il Movimento artistico-letterario **Immagine & Poesia** al Teatro Alfa di Torino, un movimento che si è rapidamente diffuso in tutto il mondo attraverso il web e attraverso mostre in Italia e all'estero, un movimento che è stato accolto favorevolmente da artisti, poeti e critici di diversi paesi e che oggi conta centinaia di sostenitori.

Questo libro vuole essere un piccolo esempio di come la poesia possa ispirare l'arte figurativa e viceversa e di come le due forme espressive una volta unite possano dare origine ad una nuova opera ricca e completa.

Ulteriori numerosi esempi sono riportati nel sito del Movimento:

www.immaginepoesia.org

"Poetry and figurative art lead to moments of cross fertilization"

When British writer **Aeronwy Thomas** (**Dylan Thomas**' daughter) said these words during her visit to Turin in 2006, nobody could really imagine how far this assertion would lead.

The following year the artistic-literary Movement **Immagine & Poesia** was born at Torino Teatro Alfa and within a few years the Movement rapidly spread via the Web, where collaborations between artists and poets are published, as well as through international exhibitions. Today it includes hundreds of artists and poets from all over the world.

This book is meant as the example of how a poem can inspire the artist or a painting can be the source of inspiration for the poet with the result of a new work that is greater than the parts, changed and magnified by the union.

Other examples can be found in the web site of the Movement:

www.immaginepoesia.org

SECTION 1: IMMAGINE & POESIA

Immagine & Poesia *per Jackson Pollock*	**Image & Poetry** *for Jackson Pollock*
Pollock-Krasner House, East Hampton	*Pollock-Krasner House, East Hampton*
Ora finalmente posso vederti *Jackson Pollock* chino sul pavimento con bastoncini e pennelli intento a sgocciolare colori sulla tela.	Now at last I see you *Jackson Pollock* kneeling on the floor handling sticks and brushes dripping paints on your canvas.
Dalla notte scura della tua mente un universo diverso emerge	From the dark night of your mind a different universe emerges
nuove galassie (*lunghe linee che si annodano*) prendono forma	new galaxies (*long looping lines*) take form
mentre le tue mani si muovono rapide	as your hands move rapidly around
regni senza forma e senza tempo dove mi sento sprofondare sempre di più avvolta dai colori del tuo *Arcobaleno Grigio*.	formless and timeless realms where I sink deep and deeper wrapped in the colours of your *Greyed Rainbow*.
Per un po' mi fermerò ad ascoltare il silenzio dell'oceano	For a while I will linger and listen to the silence of the ocean
(*o forse il rombo del motore della tua Oldsmobile decappottabile*)	(*or maybe to the roaring motor of your Oldsmobile convertible*)
poi – questa sera – scriverò una poesia solo per te *Jackson Pollock*.	then – tonight – I will write a poem just for you *Jackson Pollock*.
2 agosto 2012	*August 2, 2012*

Adel Gorgy: Traces of Pollock No. 3

SECTION 2: C'era una volta *(L'Infanzia)* – Once Upon a time *(Childhood)*

(Poesie in ricordo di mio padre Guido Chiarelli, artefice degli impianti di illuminazione a Torino 1956 - 1968 / Poems in Memory of My Father, Guido Chiarelli, head engineer for the lighting projects in Torino 1956–1968)

An Evening Sky	An Evening Sky
A slash of Blue! A sweep of Gray! *Some scarlet patches - on the way -* *Compose an evening sky . . .* **—Emily Dickinson**	*A slash of Blue! A sweep of Gray!* *Some scarlet patches - on the way -* *Compose an evening sky . . .* **—Emily Dickinson**
Era dolce il profumo di quelle sere quando i nostri passi inventavano lunghi itinerari nei giardini d'estate	So sweet was the scent of those evenings when our steps invented long distance routes in the summer gardens
quando lentamente i lampioni si accendevano e gareggiando con la luna e le stelle formavano parabole di luce sulle pietre opache dei sentieri.	when slowly the lights were lit and competing with the moons and the s stars formed parabolas of light on the opaque stones of the paths.
La vita allora appena iniziata sembrava svelare solo per noi un cielo di colori irreali.	Then, life just begun seemed to reveal – just for us – a sky of unreal colours.
Innumerevoli immagini *(schegge di ricordi lontani)* che oggi si compongono e si frantumano nel caleidoscopio stanco della mente.	Countless images *(fragments of old memories)* that today recreate and break in the weary kaleidoscope of the mind.
(Premio *Il Meleto di Guido Gozzano*, 2012)	(*Il Meleto di Guido Gozzano* Award, 2012)

14

Gianpiero Actis: Torino di Luce

Il Giardino Incantato	The Enchanted Garden
(Flor 61)	**(Flor 61)**
I pavoni camminavano *sotto gli alberi della notte* *alla luce perduta* *della luna* **—Lawrence Ferlinghetti**	*Peacocks walked* *under the night trees* *in the lost moon* *light . . .* **—Lawrence Ferlinghetti**
E poi furono le luci che si accesero lentamente nel giardino dai mille colori.	And then there were the lights that lit slowly in the garden of a thousand colours.
Si accesero calde, vibranti sulle pietre dei viali sui petali dei tulipani sull'acqua delle fontane accarezzate da un'esile brezza.	They lit warm, vibrant on the stones of paths on the petals of tulips on the water of fountains caressed by a gentle breeze.
Le luci si accesero per me che camminavo nei sentieri fioriti mentre fragranze sottili mi avvolgevano nel silenzio della sera e le bandiere mosse dal vento diventavano forme screziate di un quadro incompiuto.	The lights switched on for me as I walked on the flowered avenues and subtle fragrances wrapped me up in the silence of the night then the flags moved by the wind became the variegated forms of an incomplete painting.
Grappolo di ricordi lontani che oggi si ricompongono mentre stringo fra le dita l'ultima, appassita rosa di maggio.	Cluster of old memories that today are recomposing while I hold tight in my fingers the last, dried rose of May.
in ricordo di mio padre, Guido Chiarelli, *in occasione del 150° anniversario dell'Unità* *d'Italia*	*in memory of my father, Guido Chiarelli,* *for the 150th Anniversary of Italian Unification*
maggio, 2011	*May, 2011*

Gianpiero Actis: Il giardino incantato

SECTION 3: STAGIONI – SEASONS

Concerto d'Inverno

E l'intera città dormiente va alla deriva . . .
come un dirigibile perduto
ignaro
dell'immenso mistero
> **—Lawrence Ferlinghetti**

Concerto d'inverno
che – come dolci note –
le gocce di pioggia
improvvisano
in questa fredda sera.

Abbaglianti
le luci delle vetrine
raccontano come sempre
le loro favole illusorie.

Noi camminiamo in silenzio
estranei, distratti
mentre la città
stranamente vuota
ci avvolge nel suo umido abbraccio.

2010

Winter Concert

And the whole city sleeping drifts . . .
like a lost airship
unconscious
of the immense mystery
> **—Lawrence Ferlinghetti**

Winter Concert
That—as sweet notes—
the raindrops
improvise
this cold evening.

Dazzling
the lights of the shop-windows
as always tell
their illusory tales.

We walk in silence
strangers, distracted
while the city
oddly empty
wraps us up in a damp embrace.

2010

Gianpiero Actis: Concerto d'inverno

Notte di Dicembre	December Night
Ho aperto la finestra su questa fredda notte di dicembre e le stelle nel silenzio ovattato che avvolge la città ancora una volta mi hanno parlato di te	I have opened the window on this cold December night and the stars in the silence which surrounds the city once again have told me of you
dicembre, 2010	*December, 2010*

Alessandro Actis : Notte di dicembre

Giardino di maggio
per Mary

My tears are like the quiet drift
Of petals from some magic rose . . .
—Dylan Thomas

Ancora cammineremo
nel giardino di maggio

(in un'ora tarda del giorno)

e respireremo
il profumo delle rose

(avvolgente e forte).

I petali stanchi
sulle pietre del sentiero
formeranno
il disegno di questo tempo incerto
che il vento seguiterà a scomporre
in un gioco impietoso.

E sarà allora che
anche le rondini

(in rapidi voli ellittici
nel cielo di perla)

torneranno a giocare
inconsapevoli
del il loro destino.

2011

Garden in May
for Mary

My tears are like the quiet drift
Of petals from some magic roses . . .
—Dylan Thomas

We will walk again
in the May garden

(at a late time of the day)

and will breathe
the scent of the roses

(embracing and strong).

The tired petals
on the stones of the path
will form
the drawing of this uncertain time
that the wind will continue to break down
in a ruthless game.

It will be the time
when
even the swallows

(in rapid elliptic flights
in the pearl sky)

come and play again
unaware
of their fate.

2011

R Gopakumar: Kali Yuga (The Strife Era)

Pioggia d'Agosto

Nel mio giardino triste ulula il vento,
cade l'acquata a rade goccie, poscia
più precipite giù crepita scroscia
a fili interminabili d'argento . . .
—**Guido Gozzano**

Profumo di muschio
e di fiori
che il temporale esalta

in questo pomeriggio di agosto.

I rami contorti dei meli
piangono lacrime
di una storia antica.

Mentre cammino nel viale
tra le margherite disfatte

(petali come coriandoli bagnati)

ascolto la musica struggente
che il ritmo della pioggia
compone lentamente
solo per me.

2011
Agliè, Villa il Meleto

August Rain

Nel mio giardino triste ulula il vento,
cade l'acquata a rade goccie, poscia
più precipite giù crepita scroscia
a fili interminabili d'argento . . .
—**Guido Gozzano**

Scent of musk
and flowers
that the storm enhances

this August afternoon.

The twisted branches of the apple trees
weep tears
of ancient history.

As I walk along the path
among the faded daisies

(petals like wet confetti)

I listen to the longing music
that the rhythm of the rain
slowly composes
only for me.

2011
Agliè, Villa Il Meleto

Gianpiero Actis: Pioggia d'agosto, Villa il Meleto

SECTION 4: IL RITMO DELLA VITA – THE RHYTHM OF LIFE

Il Riposo delle Barche
per Gianpiero

Abbiamo attraversato il mare
occhi
abbagliati dalla luce
labbra
aride di sale.
Mete non programmate
si delineavano davanti a noi
quando
forti e sicuri
partivamo a sfidare il vento.

Momenti sbriciolati
del passato
evanescenti e fragili
che ora
si dissolvono
come le nostre orme sulla sabbia.

2009

The Rest of the Boats
for Gianpiero

We have crossed the sea
eyes
dazzled by the light
lips
arid with salt.
Unplanned destinations
stood out in front of us
when
strong and safe
we left to challenge the wind.

Crumbled moments
of past times
evanescent and fragile
which now
fade away
as our footprints in the sand.

2009

Marsha Solomon: Boats

Colori d'Ombra	Colors of Shadow
Luci, ombre modulano liquide trasparenze in una danza lenta:	Lights, shadows modulate liquid transparencies in a slow dance:
gocce di mare adagiate su schegge di ghiaccio e preziosi fiori di smeraldo accesi da bagliori di fuoco.	ocean blue drops fallen on ice shafts and precious emerald flowers lit with fire sparks.
Un turbinio di colori che si accendono e spengono nel silenzio del giorno che passa.	A whirl of colors that switch on and off silently at the end of the day.
2010	*2010*
(poesia ispirata al portfolio di Adel Gorgy **Colors of Shadow)**	*(inspired by Adel Gorgy's Portfolio* **Colors of Shadow)**

Adel Gorgy: Translucencies in Blue

Mondo senza Tempo

Sguardi
su un mondo senza tempo
dove
creature silenziose fluttuano e si perdono
in un mare di cristallo

e
gocce di colore si posano
adagio
su veli di ghiaccio

lampioni antichi
frammenti di luce
filtrata dal buio della notte

2008

(poesia ispirata ai quadri di Gianpiero Actis – serie
Floating Eyes)

Timeless World

Glances towards
a world without time
where silent creatures
float and lose themselves
in a sea of crystal

and
drops of colour settle
slowly
on veils of ice

street lamps
from times past
splinters of light
filter through
the dark night

2008

Translated by Aeronwy Thomas

(inspired by Gianpiero Actis' ***Floating Eyes***
series of paintings)

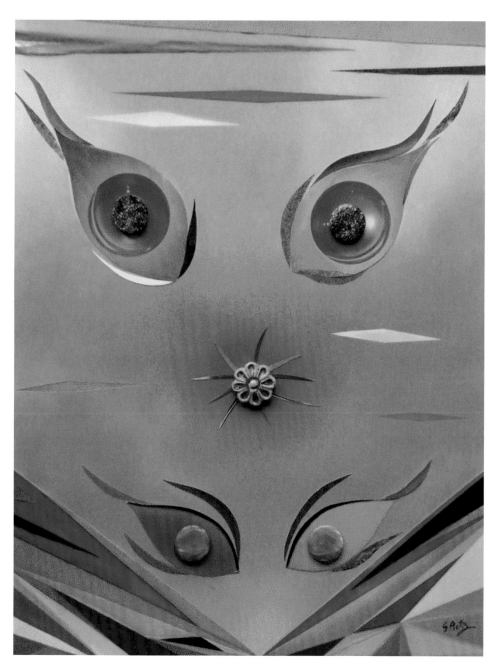

Gianpiero Actis: Floating Eyes

SECTION 5: TRAVEL DIARY

Jones Beach, summer afternoon
per Adel, Mary, and Marsha

We were together. I forget the rest.
        —Walt Whitman

I gabbiani inventavano
spirali di luce
nel pomeriggio assolato a Jones Beach.

Leggero il vento dell'Atlantico
increspava l'acqua di perla.

Abbiamo respirato
il forte profumo di salsedine
lo sguardo perso nell'orizzonte lontano.

Improvvisi – sulla sabbia impalpabile –
ci hanno accarezzato
sogni di felicità.

27 luglio 2010, Long Island

Jones Beach, summer afternoon
for Adel, Mary, and Marsha

We were together. I forget the rest.
        —Walt Whitman

The seagulls invented
spirals of light
in the sunny afternoon at Jones Beach.

Gentle, the Atlantic wind
rippled the pearl water.

We have breathed
the salty tang of the sea
our eyes lost in the far horizon.

On the intangible sand
sudden dreams of happiness
have touched us lightly.

July 27, 2010, Long Island

Adel Gorgy: Here We Walked

Times Square

Accendetevi
accendetevi ancora una volta
luci di Times Square.

*Accendetevi per me
in questa ultima sera a New York.*

L'aria calda delle strade è un manto leggero
che mi avvolge.

Come girandole in perenne movimento
non fermate la vostra danza.

Lasciate che i miei occhi
si perdano
ancora
nel vostro vortice
dolce
e inebriante.

26 luglio 2010

Times Square

Switch on
switch on once more
lights at Times Square.

*Switch on for me
in my last night in New York.*

The hot air in the streets is a gentle cloak
that wraps me up.

Like windmills moving and moving
don't stop your dance.

Let my eyes get lost
again
into your
whirl
so sweet
so intoxicating.

26 July, 2010

Alessandro Actis: Times Square Lights

Empire State Building

Viola il cielo del tramonto
in questo pomeriggio estivo
dall'Empire State Building.

La dinamica geometria della città
si svela
davanti a me
lentamente.

Lontana
quasi irraggiungibile
sento pulsare la vita nelle strade
mentre
innumerevoli luci
si accendono
poco alla volta
sul teatro del mondo.

24 luglio 2010, New York

Empire State Building

Purple, the sunset sky
this summer afternoon
from the Empire State Building.

The dynamic geometry of the city
opens
in front of me
slowly.

I can feel the streets throb with life
– far
almost unreachable –
while
innumerable lights
switch on
little by little
in the world theatre.

July 24, 2010, New York

36

Adel Gorgy: Empire State Building

Manhattan

I grattacieli si proiettano
verso le nuvole
che corrono veloci
nel cielo indaco e rosa
di un mattino di luglio.

Schegge di luce
riflessa sui cristalli di Manhattan

Al risveglio della città
voci e colori
si mescolano
nell'inquieta giostra della vita.

24 luglio 2010, New York

Manhattan

The skyscrapers soar
into the clouds
that swiftly run
in the indigo and pink sky
this July morning.

Shafts of light
reflect on the crystals of Manhattan.

The city awakes
voices and colours
mix
in the restless carousel of life.

July 24, 2010, New York

Alessandro Actis: Manhattan

Circle Line

Others will enter the gates of the ferry and
cross from shore to shore . . .
Others will see the shipping of Manhattan north
and west . . .
                            —Walt Whitman

Scivola adagio
sulle acque dell'East River
la barca che ci porta a
Ellis Island.

Il vapore del temporale estivo
sugli edifici di Brooklyn e di Queens
è una nebbia sottile
che attutisce gli scarsi rumori
di una domenica d'estate.

Miraggio di un mondo nuovo
irreale come in un sogno
la Statua della Libertà
solleva la fiaccola verso un cielo di piombo.

Anch'io, America, voglio vivere il tuo sogno.

26 luglio 2010, New York

Circle Line

Others will enter the gates of the ferry and
cross from shore to shore . . .
Others will see the shipping of Manhattan north
and west . . .
                            —Walt Whitman

The boat that takes us to
Ellis Island
slowly glides
on the water of the East River.

The haze of the summer storm
on the buildings of Brooklyn and of Queens
is a thin mist
that muffles the noise
already weak
on a summer Sunday.

Mirage of a new world
unreal like in a dream
the Statue of Liberty
raises her torch towards a leaden sky.

I, too, America, want to live your dream.

26 July, 2010, New York

Adel Gorgy: Statue of Liberty

Central Park

I have heard the sound of summer
in the rain
—Lawrence Ferlinghetti

Il ritmato suono di un blues
a **Central Park**
modula i miei pensieri
mentre percorro
il sentiero verso
Strawberry Fields.

In lontananza
- filtrata da una leggera pioggia estiva -
appare la finestra del Dakota Building
che si è chiusa
una gelida sera di dicembre.

Perfetto nella sua geometria
un cerchio di mosaico bianco e nero
racchiude
un'unica parola:
Imagine

le mie dita sfiorano
quel messaggio di pace

ancora qui
nonostante tutto

25 luglio 2010, New York

Central Park

I have heard the sound of summer
in the rain
—Lawrence Ferlinghetti

A blues beat
at **Central Park**
modulates my thoughts
as I walk
the path to
Strawberry Fields.

Far away
– filtered through the light summer rain –
a window of The Dakota
appears
a window that was closed
long ago
in a freezing-cold December evening.

Perfect in its geometry
a white and black mosaic circle
holds
one word only:
Imagine

my fingers softly touch
that message of peace

still here
in spite of all

July 25, 2010, New York

Adel Gorgy: Central Park

Tiffany

Diamonds are forever
—Ian Fleming

La porta scorrevole
si spalanca silenziosa e invitante
Welcome to Tiffany
la Grotta di Aladino
del nuovo secolo.
L'afa di questo pomeriggio d'estate
è ormai alla mie spalle.

Una morbida moquette rosa
accoglie i miei passi
mai così felpati
mentre il ronzio del condizionatore
diventa una dolce musica.

Mi aggiro con circospezione
fra le scintillanti vetrine
gioielli di raffinato design
occhieggiano.

Going up?
Il ragazzo dell'ascensore
mi invita gentilmente.

Al secondo piano
diamanti *solitaire*
con taglio *marquise*
raccontano fiabe lontane
di maharajahs e regine.

Going up?
Gift department.
Una commessa, dal fare elegante,
ripone in un sacchetto *azzurro-Tiffany*
i regali che in Italia si aspettano da me
e mi sorride.

Anch'io sorrido:
come nuova Audrey Hepburn
da oggi sono entrata
nella leggenda di **Tiffany.**

25 luglio 2010, New York

Tiffany

Diamonds are forever
—Ian Fleming

The sliding door
opens wide, quiet and appealing
Welcome to Tiffany
the Aladdin's cave
of the Twenty-first century.
The sultriness of this summer afternoon
is already behind me.

A soft pink carpet
is ready for my steps
– ever so stealthy –
while the humming of the air conditioning
becomes a sweet tune.

I cautiously hang about
among the shining display cabinets
jewels with refined designs
peep out.

Going up?
The lift boy
invites me kindly.

On the second floor
solitaire diamonds
– *marquise* cut –
tell distant tales
of maharajahs and queens.

Going up?
Gift department.
A very smart shop assistant
puts the presents
– which in Italy they expect from me –
into a *Tiffany-blue* bag
and smiles.

I'm smiling too, now:
like a new Audrey Hepburn
today I have become part of
Tiffany's legend.

July 25, 2010, New York

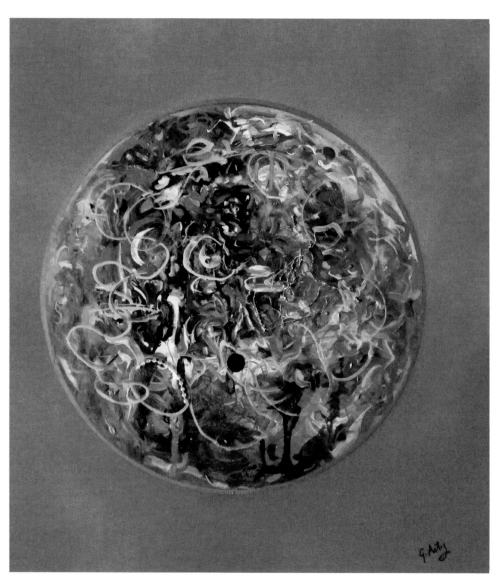

Gianpiero Actis: Tiffany (Pollock's style)

Coney Island

. . . or a joker in a straw
putting a stickpin in his peppermint tie
and looking just like he had nowhere to go
but coneyisland . . .
—Lawrence Ferlinghetti

Andiamo a Coney Island
oggi i cancelli si aprono per noi,
l'odore di salsedine
permea l'aria calda di agosto.
Entriamo, dimentichiamo
per un'ora soltanto
i problemi e gli affanni della vita.

Una girandola
di suoni e di colori fluorescenti
ci attira
calamita inebriante.

Andiamo.
La ruota panoramica
ci porterà sempre più in alto,
il nostro sguardo accarezzerà la città
e si perderà nel blu dell'oceano.

Vedremo
i cavalli delle giostre
girare in una instancabile danza.

Sentiremo
diffondersi adagio nell'aria
il dolce profumo di zucchero filato.

Un magico regno ci aspetta
per trasportarci lontano
attraverso il tempo e lo spazio:

oggi andiamo a Coney Island
e per un'ora soltanto
torneremo bambini.

3 agosto 2012

Coney Island

. . . or a joker in a straw
putting a stickpin in his peppermint tie
and looking just like he had nowhere to go
but coneyisland . . .
—Lawrence Ferlinghetti

Let's go to Coney Island
today the gates are open for us
the hot August air
is laden with saltiness.
Let's enter and forget
just for an hour
the problems and troubles of life.

A windmill
of sounds and fluorescent colours
attracts us
intoxicating magnet.

We go.
The Wonder Wheel
will take us high and higher
our eyes will caress the city
and will get lost into the blue of the ocean.

We see
the carousel horses
moving in a tireless dance.

We smell
the sweet aroma of cotton candy
slowly spreading in the air.

A magic realm is waiting
to take us far
through time and space:

today let's go to Coney Island
and just for an hour
we will be children again.

August 3, 2012

Alessandro Actis: Coney Island

Niagara

Nothing is softer or more flexible than water
yet nothing can resist it.
—**Lao Tzu** (nato nel 604 aC)

Avanziamo sul fiume
ondeggia la barca sulle acque ribollenti
ed è come sentire
il respiro delle onde.

Una pioggia sottile ci accarezza
il fragore sempre più forte
è musica di tempi antichi.

Avvolti da una nebbia leggera
rabbrividiamo di fronte all'abisso

(il nostro sguardo
abbraccia
il vortice impazzito)

e lentamente ci perdiamo
nell'incomparabile candore
delle cascate del Niagara.

27 luglio 2012

Niagara

Nothing is softer or more flexible than water
yet nothing can resist it.
—**Lao Tzu** (born 604 BC)

We advance on the river
the boat rocks on the seething waters
and it is like hearing
the waves' breath.

A gentle rain caresses us
the roar—strong and stronger—
is music from ancient times.

Enshrouded by a soft mist
we shiver in front of the abyss

(our glance
embraces
the frenzied whirlpool)

and slowly we merge into the
fathomless whiteness
of Niagara falls.

July 27, 2012

Alessandro Actis: Niagara

Boston

per Alessandro

. . . E hai passeggiato di notte sulle colline . . .
A mezzogiorno hai camminato nella luce,
Assaporando la mia stessa gioia.
—Dylan Thomas

Bianche vele
scivolano
sul fiume Charles
e riflessi dorati
vanno alla deriva
sull'acqua turchese.

I grattacieli di vetro
si immergono
nella pigra corrente.

Dal ponte
il tuo sguardo
è attento a cogliere i segreti della città
e le tue dita
– leggere sulla macchina fotografica –
sono pronte a fermare il momento che fugge.

Ora so che
attraverso le tue immagini
non finirà
questa calda estate
ancora ci abbaglierà la sua luce.
ancora ci parlerà il suo pacato silenzio.

dal Longfellow Bridge, 31 luglio 2012

Boston

for Alessandro

. . . And you have walked upon the hills at night . . .
When it was noon have walked into the light,
Knowing such joy as I.
—Dylan Thomas

White sailboats
glide
on the Charles river
and golden reflections
drift
on the turquoise water.

The glass skyscrapers
toe
the idle current.

From the bridge
your glance
is attentive to discover the secrets of the town
and your fingers
– light on the camera –
are ready to catch the fleeting moment.

Now I know that
through your images
this hot summer
will never end
we will be dazzled by its light again
and again its deep silence will speak to us.

from Longfellow Bridge, July 31, 2012

Alessandro Actis: Boston from Longfellow Bridge

SECTION 6: FOR A FRIEND

Poesia per Aeronwy Thomas

Luminosa e pura
la luce della tua stella
in questa sera d'estate
è un luccichio lieve
che si riflette
sull'estuario del Taff.

Pagine aperte
sfogliate dal vento.

Le tue parole
restano qui

ancora e sempre

e diventano
immagini e dolci melodie
cullate adagio
dal respiro del mare.

28 luglio 2009

Poem for Aeronwy Thomas

So bright and pure
the light of your star
on this summer night
is a gentle twinkling
reflected
on the Taff estuary.

Open pages
which the wind turns over.

Your words
are

still and always here

to create
images and soft tunes
lulled slowly
by the breath of the Welsh sea.

July 28, 2009

Carolyn Mary Kleefeld: Cerulean Shorelines

ARTWORKS

Gianpiero Actis: *Pollock's Eye*, mixed-media, 2012 (front cover)

N. 1   **Adel Gorgy**: *Traces of Pollock No. 3*, fine art photo, 2012
N. 2   **Gianpiero Actis**: *Torino di Luce*, mixed-media, 2008
N. 3   **Gianpiero Actis**: *Il giardino incantato*, mixed-media, 2012
N. 4   **Gianpiero Actis**: *Concerto d'inverno*, mixed-media, 2012
N. 5   **Alessandro Actis**: *Notte di dicembre*, fine art photo, 2009
N. 6   **R Gopakumar**: *Kali Yuga (The Strife Era)*, digital print, 2013
N. 7   **Gianpiero Actis**: *Pioggia d'agosto, Villa il Meleto*, acrylic colors on canvas, 2012
N. 8   **Marsha Solomon**: *Boats*, pen-and-ink, 2012
N. 9   **Adel Gorgy**: *Translucencies in Blue*, fine art photo, 2011
N. 10   **Gianpiero Actis:** *Floating Eyes*, mixed-media, 2007
N. 11   **Adel Gorgy**: *Here We Walked*, fine art photo, 2010
N. 12   **Alessandro Actis**: *Times Square Lights*, fine art photo, 2012
N. 13   **Adel Gorgy**: *Empire State Building*, fine art photo, 2010
N. 14   **Alessandro Actis**: *Manhattan*, fine art photo, 2012
N. 15   **Adel Gorgy**: *Circle Line*, fine art photo, 2012
N. 16   **Adel Gorgy**: *Central Park*, fine art photo, 2010
N. 17   **Gianpiero Actis**: *Tiffany (Pollock's Style)*, mixed-media, 2012
N. 18   **Alessandro Actis**: *Niagara*, fine art photo, 2012
N. 19   **Alessandro Actis**: *Boston from Longfellow Bridge*, fine art photo, 2012
N. 20   **Alessandro Actis**: *Coney Island*, fine art photo, 2012
N. 21   **Carolyn Mary Kleefeld**: *Cerulean Shorelines*, mixed-media, 1989
N. 22   **Lidia Chiarelli**: *Poetry Tree – Agliè,* Installation, 2012

Gianpiero Actis – Lidia Chiarelli: Logo of Immagine & Poesia, 2007 (Page 2)

Artists' sites

Alessandro Actis:	http://alessandroactis.jimdo.com/
Gianpiero Actis:	http://gianpieroactis.jimdo.com/
R Gopakumar:	http://www.gopakumarartgallery.com/
Adel Gorgy:	http://adelgorgy.com/
Carolyn Mary Kleefeld:	http://www.carolynmarykleefeld.com/
Marsha Solomon:	http://marshasolomon.com/

L'AUTRICE - ABOUT THE AUTHOR

Lidia Chiarelli: scrittrice, artista, ideologa e socio-fondatore del Movimento artistico letterario **Immagine & Poesia.** Conseguita la laurea in Lingue e Letterature straniere presso l'Università di Torino, si dedica all'insegnamento della lingua inglese, inserendo nei suoi metodi di insegnamento corsi di "scrittura creativa" abbinata all'arte. Organizza una mostra di *Mail Art* presso la scuola media G. Perotti di Torino (1990) ed è questa l'occasione per fare la conoscenza di diversi artisti, tra cui **Sarah Jackson**, *digital artist* di Halifax. La collaborazione a distanza con l'artista canadese e con la scrittrice inglese **Aeronwy Thomas** (figlia del poeta Dylan Thomas), la portano a fondare, con altri quattro soci, il Movimento artistico-letterario **Immagine & Poesia** (2007). Da una visita al **MoMA** di New York nel 2010 trae l'idea di diffondere installazioni simili al *Wish Tree* di Yoko Ono, appendendo ad alberi o a rami colorati poesie e cartoncini artistici : le installazioni di Lidia Chiarelli cominciano così a comparire in occasione di diverse mostre in Piemonte e all'estero. Le sue poesie, nate dalla passione per la scrittura creativa, hanno ottenuto importanti riconoscimenti (come le segnalazioni di merito a Swansea – Wales - *First International Poetry Festival*, 2011 e ad Agliè – Torino - *Premio Il Meleto di Guido Gozzano* 2011 e 2012), sono state tradotte in inglese, francese e rumeno (Dr. Olimpia Jacob) e sono state pubblicate su riviste e siti-web di poesia in Italia, Gran Bretagna, Stati Uniti e in Romania.

Lidia Chiarelli was born and raised in Turin, in northern Italy, where she studied and graduated in "English Language and Literature" at the University of Torino. For several years, she devoted herself to teaching English in secondary schools, and included "creative expression" courses in her teaching methods. She organized a unique *"mail art"* exhibition at Giuseppe Perotti School (Torino, 1990), which turned out to be an opportunity to become acquainted with many artists, especially with *Sarah Jackson,* a digital artist from Halifax, Canada. Her long distance collaboration with the Canadian artist, Jackson, and with British writer *Aeronwy Thomas*, (the daughter of *Dylan Thomas*), led her to found, with four other members, the artistic literary Movement **Immagine & Poesia**, which was officially presented at *Alfa Teatro* of Torino on Novembre 9, 2007. After visiting the *Museum of Modern Art* in New York in 2010, Lidia was inspired to create installations similar to Yoko Ono's *Wish Tree*, but hanging not only wishes, but poems and original works of art on cards on the trees. Lidia Chiarelli's *"Poetry&Art Trees"* thus began to appear in different exhibitions in Piedmont and abroad. Lidia's passion for creative writing has motivated her to write poetry, and she became an award-winning poet in 2011 and 2012 : *Premio Il Meleto di Guido Gozzano*, Agliè 2011 (Segnalazione di Merito) and 2012 (Terzo Premio poesia inedita). In June 2011 she was awarded a Certificate of Appreciation from *The First International Poetry Festival of Swansea* (U.K.) for her broadside poetry and art contribution. Her writing has been translated into English, French, and Romanian (Dr. Olimpia Jacob) and published in poetry reviews and on websites in Italy, Great Britain, in the U.S.A. and in Romania.

http://lidiachiarelli.jimdo.com/
http://www.worldart.info/LidiaChiarelliBio-Data.asp
e mail: immagine.poesia@gmail.com

Lidia Chiarelli: Poetry Tree – Agliè